PRO WRESTLING LEGENDS

CHELSEA HOUSE PUBLISHERS

PRO WRESTLING LEGENDS

Lex Luger:
The Story of the Wrestler
They Call "The Total Package"

Jacqueline Mudge

Chelsea House Publishers
Philadelphia

Produced by Chestnut Productions and Choptank Syndicate, Inc.

Editor and Picture Researcher: Mary Hull
Design and Production: Lisa Hochstein

CHELSEA HOUSE PUBLISHERS

Editor in Chief: Sally Cheney
Associate Editor in Chief: Kim Shinners
Production Manager: Pamela Loos
Art Director: Sara Davis
Director of Photography: Judy L. Hasday
Cover Illustrator: Keith Trego

Cover Photos: Sports Action and
                    Jeff Eisenberg Sports Photography

The Chelsea House World Wide Web site
address is http://www.chelseahouse.com

First Printing

1 3 5 7 9 8 6 4 2

Library of Congress Cataloging-in-Publication Data

Mudge, Jacqueline.
    Lex Luger: the story of the wrestler they call
    "the Total Package / Jacqueline Mudge.
        p. cm. — (Pro wrestling legends)
    Includes bibliographical references (p.) and index.
    ISBN 0–7910–6448–4 (alk. paper) — ISBN 0–7910–6449–2 (pbk. : alk. paper)
        1. Luger, Lex—Juvenile literature. 2. Wrestlers—United States—Juvenile literature.
    [1. Luger, Lex. 2. Wrestlers.] I. Title. II. Series.

GV1196.L84 M83 2001
796.812'092—dc21
[B]
                                                                              00–069413

Contents

1 THE FIRST WORLD TITLE

When Lex Luger stepped into the ring for the main event of the Great American Bash on July 4, 1991, he knew that he had the best chance of his life to win the World Championship Wrestling (WCW) World heavyweight title. He had been so close before, and now he was closer than ever. The belt had eluded him so many times before, but this time his opponent wasn't all-time great Ric Flair. It was Barry Windham, a man who over the years had been both his friend and his opponent.

Luger was expecting Ric Flair to be his opponent, but Flair had been stripped of the championship. Despite the change, however, Luger knew not to count the belt won until Windham submitted or was pinned.

"I've taken on Flair so many times for the title, I've come to know what to expect from him," Luger told *Pro Wrestling Illustrated Weekly*. "But Barry is a totally different kind of competitor. I've had to change my mode of training and strategy completely. I have no doubt under these circumstances, this is going to be the toughest match of my entire career. In a way, it's like being a contender for an entirely new title."

The match for the vacant world title took place at the Baltimore Arena, the scene of a mishap for Luger three years

A triumphant Lex Luger raises the WCW World heavyweight belt over his head after winning the championship for the first time.

Barry Windham was a formidable competitor, but he could not stop Lex Luger from winning his first WCW World title.

earlier. In 1988, in the main event of the Great American Bash, Luger thought he had Flair beaten when he lifted the world champion into his "torture rack" backbreaker. Flair was grimacing in pain when, suddenly, the referee stopped the bout. Incredibly, though, Luger wasn't declared the winner. An official of the Maryland State Athletic Commission stopped the bout because of an open cut on Luger's forehead.

This time, Luger had a surprise for the crowd in Baltimore and those watching at home on pay-per-view television. Harley Race, the seven-time former National Wrestling Alliance (NWA) and World Championship Wrestling (WCW) World champion known for his rulebreaking tactics, accompanied him to the ring. With Race was Mr. Hughes, a bodyguard.

Windham came to the ring by himself.

Shortly after the opening bell, Windham rocked Luger with a dropkick, but Luger got up, pounded Windham to the mat, and backed up Windham with a series of right hands. Windham responded by backdropping Luger to the mat, but Luger blocked Windham's vertical suplex and came back with one of his own. Luger escaped a figure-four leglock, a painful submission hold made popular by Ric Flair in which the attacker locks up his opponent's legs, putting incredible strain on the upper thighs and lower back. Luger weakened Windham with a spinecrusher and a tackle, then locked Windham in a sleeperhold. Windham worked his way out and put a sleeper on Luger, who managed to escape.

Now both men were on a rampage. Luger floored Windham with a DDT and scored a two-count. Windham knocked Luger off the top rope and scored a two-count of his own. Luger back-dropped Windham, then nearly took his opponent's breath away with three devastating clotheslines. Luger covered Windham for the pin, but got only a two-count.

The match was only 10 minutes old, but both men were exhausted from the nonstop pace. Luger bodyslammed Windham, then placed him in the torture rack. Windham screamed as he was held high above Luger's head, but he executed a brilliant flip to get out of trouble. Windham scored with two clotheslines and covered Luger for a two-count, then nearly got a three-count after a dropkick from the top rope. Luger was in trouble. He conferred with Race and Hughes.

"Now's the time," Race told him.

Luger turned around and kneed Windham into the turnbuckle. Then he scored with a piledriver, a lethal move in which the attacker places his opponent's head between his thighs, lifts his body perpendicular to the canvas, then drives his head into the mat. Windham was helpless. Luger covered Windham. The referee made the three-count.

Luger had won his first WCW World heavyweight title. "This is the dawning of the era of the 'Total Package,'" Luger said afterwards. It had been six long years in coming.

The wrestler who would come to be known as Lex Luger was born Larry Pfhol on June 2, 1958, in Chicago. His father was involved in the retail music business and real estate. The family lived in two other cities during Larry's childhood: Buffalo, New York, and Boca Raton, Florida.

Growing up in Buffalo, Larry was a standout athlete in football, basketball, and track. He continued starring in sports when he and his family moved to Florida. Always a big person—he would peak in size at 6' 5", 265 pounds—Luger dominated the smaller, less mature athletes on the other teams. Anybody who watched him play back then had no doubt that he would one day make a living as a professional athlete.

Pfhol attended the University of Florida on a football scholarship and played offensive guard. He always played basketball and wrestled in college, but when he was 19 years old, Pfhol was kicked off the football team for bad behavior. He immediately contacted teams in the Canadian Football League, despite the coach of the University of Florida team telling Larry he didn't have enough experience to make a professional team. The young athlete was intent on proving his coach wrong. He

Wearing a football uniform, Lex Luger, at right, stands with Giants player Lawrence Taylor. Luger played for several football teams before making his professional wrestling debut with Florida Championship Wrestling (FCW) in 1985.

quit school, headed north to Canada, and had a tryout with the Montreal Alouettes. Pfhol made the team.

Pfhol played three seasons as offensive tackle for the Alouettes from 1979 to 1981, playing in 14 games, until he became eligible for the National Football League (NFL). He signed with the Green Bay Packers as an offensive guard, but never played in a game. He jumped to the United States Football League (USFL) in 1984 and played for the Memphis Showboats until 1985, when he decided to quit football.

"You can use football or let it use you," said Luger, who was fortunate never to have suffered an injury in football.

At the time, Pfhol was living in an apartment in Tampa, Florida, during the off-season. In early 1985, he was playing in a celebrity golf tournament near Tampa when he met Bob Roop, a former wrestler popular in the Florida area. Roop introduced Pfhol to trainer Hiro Matsuda, who convinced Pfhol to try wrestling.

Under the tutelage of Roop and Matsuda, who had a reputation as one of the finest trainers in the sport, Pfhol learned quickly. He changed his name to Lex Luger and on October 31, 1985, he made his pro debut against Ed "the Bull" Gantner on a Florida Championship Wrestling (FCW) card at the Daytona Beach Ocean Center. Luger won.

Nineteen days later, on November 19, 1985, Luger was given the opportunity of a lifetime: a title match against southern champion Wahoo McDaniel, a veteran wrestler who had worked in every major federation in North America. Luger beat McDaniel for the belt and immediately gained recognition in the wrestling world.

Several national wrestling magazines called Luger "the next Hulk Hogan."

Luger proved his victory was not a fluke by winning several rematches. He and Roop also feuded with Barry and Kendall Windham, two fan favorites in Florida. Luger showed his temper for the first time on January 15, 1986, when he lost the title to Art Barr in Tampa and reacted by tearing apart the locker room. Luger regrouped, regaining the title by beating Barry Windham on February 14 in Orlando.

News of this spectacular muscleman with the hot temper and the impressive brawling skills spread quickly. Even though he had been wrestling for less than six months, Luger was already considered a top contender for the sport's major titles. In the mid-1980s, FCW was

As one of FCW's top wrestlers, Luger was occasionally granted a match against National Wrestling Alliance World champion Ric "Nature Boy" Flair, who became his nemesis.

affiliated with the National Wrestling Alliance (NWA), and FCW's top wrestlers occasionally got shots at the NWA World title, one of the most prestigious championships in the world. Luger got several shots at NWA World champ Ric Flair.

On May 14, 1986, Luger appeared to have Flair pinned, but the champ had his foot on the ropes and the referee called for a break. Luger dominated the rest of the match, and Flair had to save himself by getting disqualified.

Luger became a fan favorite in Florida when he befriended Windham in late May. A few weeks later in Orlando, Luger and Flair battled once again, this time in a best-of-three-falls match for Flair's NWA World title. Luger won the first fall and appeared to be on his way to winning the world championship when manager Sir Oliver Humperdink's men attacked Luger during the break between the first and second falls. They injured Luger, who had to be rushed to a hospital for treatment.

Luger's second southern title reign ended on July 22, 1986, when he lost to Masked Superstar in a controversial match. Superstar pulled a foreign object out of his mask, struck Luger, and scored the pin. But Luger's third title reign started just one week later, when he pinned Superstar.

Luger got better each week. He and Flair hooked up again in another best-of-three-falls match on September 1, 1986. Luger lost the first fall, but battled back to win the second fall with a reverse cradle. The third fall was a classic. Flair and Luger battled until the 60-minute time limit expired. Flair had barely escaped with his title.

"This is a man with unlimited potential," Roop boasted to *Pro Wrestling Illustrated* magazine. "Lex can be the world champion anywhere he wrestles, and he's already proven his dominance in Florida. This is a man who is going to rule the sport for the rest of the 1980s, and all of the 1990s!" The fans certainly agreed. The readers of *Pro Wrestling Illustrated* named Luger Rookie of the Year for 1986 by an overwhelming margin.

In his first year, Luger won three southern titles, took the world champion to the limit several times, and proved beyond any doubt that he had outgrown FCW. Early in 1987, Luger lost the southern title to Kevin Sullivan, broke his ties with Roop, and signed with the NWA. He was now Lex Luger, the "Total Package."

Since their formation in May 1986, the Four Horsemen had become the most powerful clique in wrestling. The group consisting of Ric Flair, Tully Blanchard, Arn Anderson, Ole Anderson, and manager J.J. Dillon wreaked havoc on the NWA, much in the same way the New World Order (NWO) would 10 years later.

Ignoring his friend Barry Windham's advice, Luger wanted to join the Horsemen when he arrived in the NWA. But there was a problem: the Four Horsemen already had four wrestlers. Instead of joining the Horsemen, Luger became a Horseman "associate." It was like a tryout for the group. Luger had to prove his loyalty and worthiness. He passed the tryout, and when Ole Anderson was kicked out of the group for disloyalty, Luger became an official member.

With Luger, the Horsemen had the best young star in the world to go along with the best veteran star in the world, Ric Flair. In April, Luger teamed with Blanchard in the Jim Crockett Senior Memorial Cup Tag Team Tournament in Baltimore. The tournament brought together the best teams in the world for a two-day competition, with a $1 million first prize at stake. Luger and Blanchard beat the M.O.D. Squad in the second round. They beat Bob and Brad Armstrong in the quarterfinals and earned a spot in the finals with a victory over Japanese stars Shohei Baba and Isao Takagi. But the Horsemen fell short in the finals, losing to the fan favorite duo of Dusty Rhodes and Nikita Koloff.

Koloff and Luger, both young stars, were natural rivals, and Koloff had something that Luger wanted. Luger got what he wanted at the Great American Bash on July 11, 1987: the U.S. title, when he pinned Nikita Koloff. As U.S.

Luger carried on a 1987 feud with Nikita Koloff, left, another rising National Wrestling Alliance star.

champion, Luger was now the number one contender to the world title. But, of course, he wasn't going to get a shot at the world title because that championship was owned by his fellow Horseman, Ric Flair. Perhaps that's what the Horsemen had in mind all along when they recruited Luger: keeping him away from Flair.

Thanks to the Horsemen's help, Luger successfully defended the U.S. title in several matches against Koloff, but he was frustrated by the fact that he would never get a shot at Flair as long as he was a member of the Horsemen. Privately, Luger thought Flair should have offered him a title match, but that never happened. When Luger lost the U.S. title to Dusty Rhodes at Starrcade '87 in Chicago, he was no longer even the number one contender to the world title.

The fact was, Luger wasn't a team player. Sure, he had played on several football teams, but football is a team sport. Wrestling isn't. Luger's unwillingness to play the Horsemen's game became apparent when he and the other Horsemen, including manager J.J. Dillon, entered a battle royal. When Luger refused to throw himself over the top rope to allow Dillon to win the battle royal, he was attacked by Blanchard and Anderson.

Luger's days as a member of the Horsemen were over. His first year in the NWA had been tumultuous. The readers of *Pro Wrestling Illustrated* voted him third runner-up for Most Hated Wrestler of the Year, thanks in part to his feud with Nikita Koloff. But by the time the final vote had been counted, Luger was no longer a rulebreaker. He was a fan favorite.

3 TARGET: FLAIR

Lex Luger couldn't say that Barry Windham hadn't warned him. When Luger signed with the NWA, Windham told Luger, "Don't go near the Four Horsemen. They're only out for themselves." So when Luger was booted out of the Horsemen, Windham greeted him with open arms . . . for a while.

Luger wasted no time getting revenge against the Horsemen. On March 27, 1988, at WCW's first Clash of the Champions card, Luger and Windham beat Blanchard and Arn Anderson for the NWA World tag team title. It was a satisfying victory for Luger, who afterward declared, "They'll rue the day they ever set sight on me." But on April 20, 1988, Anderson and Blanchard regained the belts. Then Windham turned against Luger and joined the Horsemen.

Left without a partner for the 1988 Crockett Cup tournament on April 22 and 23, Luger got Sting to team with him. Although they had almost no experience wrestling with each other, they worked well together. After receiving a bye in the first round, Luger and Sting beat Dick Murdoch and Ivan Koloff. In the quarterfinals, they beat the Midnight Express. In the semifinals, they beat Barbarian and Warlord. In the championship final, they beat Tully Blanchard and Arn

By 1990 Lex Luger had won four WCW U.S. titles, but the world title continued to elude him.

Anderson. It was a spectacular victory for this newly formed tag team of young stars, who were ecstatic over winning the $1 million first prize.

With that confidence-boosting victory in hand, Luger set his sights on an old rival: "Nature Boy" Ric Flair. The Nature Boy was still NWA World champion, but Luger was confident that he could beat him. After all, he had come so close during his rookie year. Since then, Luger had gained another year of valuable experience.

Luger and Flair stepped into the ring at the Great American Bash on July 10, 1988, at the Baltimore Arena. Luger dominated the match from the opening bell, and he seemed to have Flair beaten when he lifted him into his "torture rack" backbreaker. Suddenly, the referee called for the bell. Luger thought he had won the world title. But Flair had never submitted. An official from the Maryland State Athletic Commission, sitting at ringside, had noticed that Luger was bleeding from the forehead. According to the state's rules, a match cannot continue if one wrestler is bleeding.

Irate because he felt he had been robbed of the title, Luger intensified his quest for the belt, but the Horsemen kept interfering in his matches against Flair. Hoping to prevent the Horsemen from rescuing Flair yet again, the NWA appointed former NFL star John Ayres as special referee for several bouts, but Flair still managed to hold on to the title.

"This has gone way beyond just wanting the title," Luger told *Pro Wrestling Illustrated*. "I despise Flair and everything he stands for. Joining the Horsemen was the biggest mistake of my career. I can't tell you when and where it's gonna happen, but I will be the next NWA World champion. Watch out, Flair!"

Replied Flair: "Do you really expect me to worry about that punk? If he's the number-one challenger, the 10 pounds of gold will remain around my waist for a long, long time. Even with his pal Ayres as ref, he can't win."

Luger was running out of chances. In November, Flair announced that their match at Starrcade '88 on December 26 would be Luger's last shot at the title. Luger fell short again and was pinned by Flair after 30 minutes and 59 seconds of classic action.

With the world title out of reach, Luger concentrated his efforts on the NWA's secondary belt, the U.S. title. Windham had held that belt since the previous May, and Luger had no reluctance over facing his former friend. They met at Chi-Town Rumble on February 20, 1989, in Chicago, and Luger pinned Windham in just 10:43 to begin his second U.S. title reign.

Luger lost the title to Michael Hayes on May 7 in Nashville, but regained the belt from Hayes on May 22 in West Virginia. He embarked on an ambitious series of title defenses that included a spectacular bout against rugged Steve "Dr. Death" Williams on October 7, 1989, in Pittsburgh. Luger won when he used the ropes for leverage to pin Williams. "There's no way he was beating me cleanly," Williams complained. "If he thinks he can overpower me, he's gonna have to think again. I could see the fear written all over his face. He knew he was in for a battle, and he got one."

Another challenger was Brian Pillman, the outstanding aerial wrestler known as Flyin' Brian. Luger and Pillman engaged in several scuffles during the weeks leading to their show-down at Halloween Havoc '89.

"Luger thinks he's going to teach me a lesson, but he's playing right into my hands," Pillman told *Pro Wrestling Illustrated Weekly.* "Twice now, I've taken that big man to the limits of his abilities on television. This time, I'll prove that I can beat him in a sanctioned match. Believe me, my confidence has never been greater than it is now."

At Halloween Havoc, Pillman kept Luger off-guard with an aerial assault, but made a drastic mistake: He landed right in Luger's arms after a flying bodypress. Luger dropped him throat-first on the top rope and scored the pin at 16:48 of an outstanding match.

"That punk's got a lot of nerve challenging me for this belt at this stage of his career," said Luger, who wasn't one to talk, considering how inexperienced he was when he first fought for the world title. "What really bugs me is that I've got even more matches scheduled against the guy in the weeks ahead. If he's smart, he should just pull out and forget about it."

Meanwhile, Luger had his mind on other business. At Clash of the Champions IX on November 15, 1989, in Troy, New York, Luger and the Great Muta attacked world champion Ric Flair, leaving him nearly unconscious in the middle of the ring. Luger then took a metal chair and destroyed two trophies Flair had received earlier in the evening.

Vowed Flair: "Luger had better watch his butt, because I'm gonna drive him right out of the sport."

It was a violent night for Luger, who also used a chair to beat Pillman again. A week

Mean Mark Callous, later known as the Undertaker, holds Lex Luger against the ropes during their 1990 Great American Bash match, which Luger ended up winning by pinfall.

later, Luger interfered in Flair's match against Muta and attacked Flair. But Flair was resilient. He successfully defended the title in several matches against Luger.

On December 16, 1989, in Detroit, Luger bloodied Flair's head against the ringpost, then used the ropes for leverage and pinned Flair. The referee made the three-count and Luger got up, thinking he was the new world champion, but the referee had seen Luger's feet on the ropes at the last second, and ordered the match continued. Flair went on to pin Luger.

"Luger's wasting his time," Flair said. "If he thinks he can beat me, he should try and beat me. If he thinks he has to cheat, then he doesn't belong in the same ring with me."

Responded Luger: "I'm measuring him out. I want to see how far he's fallen since last year. I think he's a shadow of the man he used to be."

Luger signed for a match against Flair at Wrestle War '90, but the Four Horsemen tried to bully him out of the match. At Wrestle War, Luger wrestled one of the best matches of his life and scored several two-counts on the champion. Late in the match, Luger caught Flair in his torture rack. Meanwhile, Ole and Arn Anderson attacked Sting, who had come to ringside to help Luger. As Ole prepared to hit Sting across his injured knee with a crutch, Luger dropped Flair and saved Sting. Luger was counted out, but Sting was grateful.

"Luger literally saved my career," Sting said.

And the Four Horsemen saved Flair from losing the title. At Capital Combat on May 19, 1990, Luger and Flair battled in a steel cage. When Ole Anderson gained entrance to the cage, the rest of the Horsemen interfered and attacked Luger, who won by disqualification but didn't get the title he coveted.

Luger's frustration over his inability to beat Flair didn't affect his performance against other opponents. He needed only 26 seconds to beat the powerful Sid Vicious at Clash of the Champions XI on June 13, 1990. He clotheslined Mark Callous and won via pinfall at the Great American Bash. Luger and Sting, who by this time had won the NWA World title, combined to beat Harley Race and Barry Windham. At Fall Brawl '90, Luger beat Flair by disqualification after getting attacked by Stan Hansen. And he solidified his friendship with Sting by watching Sting's back. But Luger's U.S. title reign ended on October 27, when he lost the belt to Hansen in Chicago.

Luger and Hansen met again in a bullrope match at Starrcade '90 in St. Louis. Bullrope matches were Hansen's specialty, and Hansen was confident of victory in the title bout. Luger won the controversial match—the referee had been knocked out—by dragging Hansen to all four corners. Luger had his fourth U.S. title, but it wasn't the title he wanted most.

WEARING THE BELT

For most pro wrestlers, not winning a world heavyweight title in the first five years of their careers wouldn't be anything to get upset about. After all, most wrestlers never win a world title. Even Ric Flair, one of the greatest champions ever, didn't win his first NWA World title until his ninth year as a pro.

Luger had been wrestling for the NWA World title since almost the first day of his career. It had always been within sight, but frustratingly out of reach. He thought there were times when he had been robbed of the belt, and other times when he should have received more title shots. Being U.S. champion was great, but Luger knew things could get better.

Not that he wasn't getting plenty of acclaim. Luger participated in 1991's Match of the Year, but it wasn't a singles match. It was a tag team bout pitting him and Sting against WCW World tag team champions Rick and Scott Steiner at SuperBrawl on May 19, 1991, in St. Petersburg. The four combatants exchanged piledrivers, leg sweeps, suplexes, and aerial clotheslines—including a devastating clothesline by Luger on Scott Steiner—before Nikita Koloff interfered. Koloff hit Sting in the face with a chain, allowing Scott Steiner to score the pin.

Lex Luger won his first WCW World title when he defeated his some-time friend, sometime enemy, Barry Windham, at the Great American Bash on July 14, 1991.

By pinning the Great Muta in only three minutes and 43 seconds at Clash of the Champions XV on June 12, 1991, in Knoxville, Tennessee, Luger earned a shot at Flair's WCW World title. Flair was having a contract dispute with WCW, however, and when the two parties couldn't reach an agreement, the federation stripped him of the title. Luger and Windham were declared the top contenders to the title.

Luger and Windham, former friends and former enemies, battled in a steel cage at the Great American Bash on July 14, 1991, in Baltimore, Maryland. On that night, Luger struck gold. With a little over 12 minutes gone in the match, he floored Windham with a piledriver, then scored the pin. For the first time, Luger was WCW World champion.

The fans weren't cheering Lex's victory, though. During the match, seven-time former WCW World champion Harley Race had come to the ring to offer Luger moral support. After the match, Luger announced that Race was his manager and Mr. Hughes was his bodyguard.

"All I needed was an attitude adjustment," Luger said. "No more worrying about the fans, no more teaming with men I didn't really like. From now on, I'll do what this man [Harley Race] tells me to do. I won't need anything else."

Luger had to give up the U.S. title because he won the world title, but he didn't care. He had the belt he wanted. Race taught Luger how to be devious, and Luger was not an honorable champion. He allowed Mr. Hughes to interfere for him in matches against Windham. On September 29, 1991, Luger and Mr. Hughes battled Windham and Ron Simmons. With

Simmons down and seemingly finished, Luger attempted to piledrive him, but Simmons back-flipped Luger, who made a tag to Windham, who knocked Race off the ring apron, after which Simmons pinned Mr. Hughes. Enraged by the loss, Luger attacked Simmons and piledrived him.

Four weeks later, Luger and Simmons met in a one-on-one match in the main event of Halloween Havoc on October 27 in Chattanooga, Tennessee. In the first fall, Simmons power-slammed and pinned Luger. The "Total Package" came back in the second fall and won by disqualification because Simmons had hurled him over the top rope. Luger won the third fall in four minutes when he piledrived Simmons and scored the pin.

Luger was first runner-up for *Pro Wrestling Illustrated* magazine's Wrestler of the Year award, but the pressure of his first world title reign quickly got to him. His rigorous travel schedule and exhausting title defenses wore him down. Luger went into seclusion to train for his match against Sting at SuperBrawl II on February 29, 1992, in Milwaukee, but exercised his mouth more than his body when the bell rang to start the match.

"You'll never beat me, not in a million years," Luger said to Sting.

"What's your problem?" Sting replied. "Do something! Come at me!"

The two settled down to battle. Sting rocked Luger with his "Stinger splash," but Luger recovered and got up, shocking the challenger. Luger responded with a clothesline that nearly tore Sting's head from his neck. Later in the match, the action spilled outside the ring, and

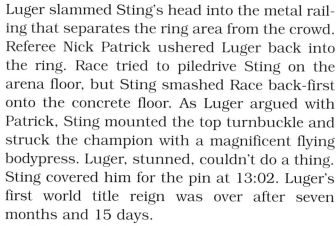

As tag team partners, Lex Luger and Sting had some memorable matches against WCW World tag team champions the Steiner brothers. Here Lex Luger pile-drives Rick Steiner during a WCW match in New York.

Luger slammed Sting's head into the metal railing that separates the ring area from the crowd. Referee Nick Patrick ushered Luger back into the ring. Race tried to piledrive Sting on the arena floor, but Sting smashed Race back-first onto the concrete floor. As Luger argued with Patrick, Sting mounted the top turnbuckle and struck the champion with a magnificent flying bodypress. Luger, stunned, couldn't do a thing. Sting covered him for the pin at 13:02. Luger's first world title reign was over after seven months and 15 days.

"Lex looked in better shape than ever, but I was just so filled with adrenaline and passion," Sting said. "The guy's sour attitude just irritated me. I really hope I taught that arrogant guy a lesson tonight."

Lesson learned? It didn't quite matter: A few days after the match, Luger shocked the wrestling world with the announcement that he was leaving WCW.

"I'm tired of the wrestling grind," Luger told *Sports Review Wrestling* magazine. "It's been very hard to take care of myself, going from town to town, night after night. It's time for me to take a breather."

Luger didn't plan to stop working. He still owned two gyms in Georgia, and he hinted that he was considering a career in bodybuilding.

"My body is always in the best condition it can possibly be," Luger said. "When I watch bodybuilding competitions, I realize that is the field I can not only compete in, but excel."

The conjecture became fact on March 28, 1992, when Luger appeared on a World Wrestling Federation (WWF) television show and announced he was switching full-time to the sport of bodybuilding as a member of the WWF-owned World Bodybuilding Federation (WBF). But the WBF was a failure, and Luger never got to compete in one of Vince McMahon's few non-wrestling ventures. On June 8, 1992, just days before he was scheduled to make his WBF debut, Luger was involved in a serious motorcycle accident. He suffered a crushed elbow, among other injuries, and was sidelined for the rest of the year.

Now Luger was not only a man without a title, he was a man without a federation. A man whose career was in trouble because of the injuries he had suffered, and the boredom he apparently felt with the sport. But perhaps the motorcycle accident was a blessing in disguise. The forced time away from the ring made him realize how much he missed wrestling.

When 1992 came to an end, Luger still hadn't returned to the ring. But when 1993 started, Luger was ready to make his entrance into the WWF.

It was not quite the entrance he would have hoped for himself.

5   THE LEX EXPRESS

L ex Luger returned to wrestling at the WWF's Royal Rumble on January 24, 1993, in Sacramento, California. He had a new manager, Bobby "the Brain" Heenan, a steel plate on his injured arm, and a new persona: he loved looking at himself in the mirror and called himself "the Narcissist." He also had a new purpose: Heenan wanted revenge against Curt Hennig for booting Ric Flair out of the WWF, and he planned to use Luger to get the job done.

Luger was thrown in immediately against the top wrestlers in the federation. He pinned Hennig at WrestleMania IX on April 4, 1993, in Las Vegas. In Providence, Rhode Island, Luger was caught in Bret Hart's sharpshooter leglock when Razor Ramon stormed the ring, attacked Hart, and saved Luger. When, during a card in Los Angeles, Ramon again interfered in a match between Hart and Luger, Luger and Ramon fought back to the dressing room. The feud between Luger and Ramon, two of the most self-centered wrestlers in the federation, heated up as the weeks went on. Luger interfered in many of Ramon's matches against Hart, too.

Through it all, though, Luger wasn't taking the WWF by storm. He was on the wrong end of the feud with Ramon. He battled to a time-limit draw with Tatanka in the first round of

Dressed in his new look as "the Narcissist" Lex Luger does his manager Bobby Heenan's bidding and clamps down on Curt Hennig.

the King of the Ring tournament, and both men were eliminated. A feud with Crush was intense, but meaningless. The fans were booing him. He was getting no closer to the WWF World title. He needed to do something big. Something that would make headlines. He soon got his chance.

Mr. Fuji, manager of Yokozuna, the 550-pound former sumo wrestler and, at the time, the WWF World champion, wanted to make America look foolish, so he planned the "Stars & Stripes Challenge" for July 4, 1993. Fuji, on behalf of Yokozuna, challenged America's finest athletes—in any sport—to a bodyslam challenge on the deck of the U.S.S. *Intrepid* battleship docked in Manhattan Harbor. Yokozuna and Mr. Fuji were convinced nobody could body-slam the champion. They appeared to be right when Yokozuna turned back the challenges of several football, basketball, and hockey players, along with several wrestlers.

The challenge was over. Fuji and Yokozuna had embarrassed America, just as they had set out to do. But just as Fuji declared the competition finished, a helicopter flew in over the ship. The helicopter landed, and out stepped Luger, wearing a red, white, and blue shirt. He stormed into the ring, pushed aside manager Bobby Heenan, and said he wanted a shot at Yokozuna.

"You're too late," said ring announcer Todd Pettingill. Luger refused to take no for an answer.

"What you are is a cancer on the WWF," Luger told Yokozuna. "Everybody wants to know what's wrong with America. There's nothing wrong with America. What's wrong with America is blood-sucking leeches like you. An over-stuffed, sushi-eating, rice-chomping wrestler we call a champion. A disgrace to the WWF. The only thing wrong with America is you, and we're going to clean house right here and right now!"

The crowd chanted "Lex! Lex! Lex!" Fuji spat on Luger, but Luger tossed him over the top rope. The crowd roared as Luger removed his shirt. Yokozuna charged at Luger, but Luger moved out of the way. Yokozuna smashed into the turnbuckle. Luger struck Yokozuna in the head with the metal plate on his right forearm—then he lifted Yokozuna and slammed him to the mat.

Wrestlers Scott Steiner and Crush, both of whom had failed to slam Yokozuna, rushed to

After bodyslamming Yokozuna on the Fourth of July in 1993, Luger toured the country on the Lex Express, proudly wearing his red, white, and blue costume.

the ring and lifted Luger on their shoulders. The crowd rejoiced. Yokozuna was incensed. Fuji claimed that Luger hadn't really slammed Yokozuna; he had merely lifted him waist high. But Fuji's claims fell on deaf ears. Luger had become an instant hero.

Luger climbed onto the Lex Express bus and went on a summer-long "Call to Action" tour of America, gaining new fans wherever he went and proclaiming himself as the patriot who would save wrestling from the evil Yokozuna and Fuji. Luger was awarded the world title match against Yokozuna at SummerSlam '93, and Jim Cornette, Yokozuna's new adviser, guaranteed that Luger would get only one chance to beat Yokozuna.

SummerSlam '93 was held on August 30 at the Palace of Auburn Hills in suburban Detroit. Late in the match, Luger leveled Yokozuna with a forearm, sending the champ careening over the ropes and to the arena floor. Yokozuna lay motionless and couldn't move while he was counted out. Since world titles can only change hands by pinfall or submission, the fact that Yokozuna had been counted out did not earn Luger the title. Luger didn't win the belt, but he won the match, scoring an important victory. Luger celebrated along with the crowd, but later was attacked in the locker room by Ludvig Borga. The next night, Luger beat intercontinental champion Shawn Michaels by countout. The Lex Express was in overdrive.

Borga, like Yokozuna, also wanted to humiliate Luger and America. He and Luger engaged in a feud that included matches in Germany, Austria, and the United States. At the Survivor Series, Luger teamed with Rick and Scott Steiner and the Undertaker to beat the international squad of Quebecer Jacques, Yokozuna, Borga, and Crush. The time had come for Luger to make another run at the WWF World title, but there was one problem: Cornette had made sure that the Summer-Slam match would be Luger's only match against Yokozuna for the world title. Luger had agreed to the stipulation. Despite losing that match by countout, Yokozuna had actually won, because he retained the belt and wouldn't have to wrestle Luger again.

But Lex found a loophole.

The Royal Rumble is one of the WWF's most unique events. Each year, on the off Sunday between the NFL's conference championships and the Super Bowl, the WWF presents this pay-per-view show in which the winner of the main event, the Royal Rumble, gets a match against the WWF World champion at WrestleMania. In the Royal Rumble, wrestlers enter the ring one at a time every two minutes. The only way to eliminate an opponent is by dumping him over the top rope to the arena floor. The last man standing is the winner.

When the WWF declared Luger eligible for the 1994 Royal Rumble, Lex realized he had his back-door entrance to another shot at Yokozuna. In reality, perhaps the WWF was bowing to popular demand. Luger had been named Most Popular Wrestler of the Year and Comeback Wrestler of the Year by *Pro Wrestling*

Lex Luger and Bret Hart, bottom, battled to a draw in their contest to see who would get the title shot against Yokozuna at WrestleMania X, so WWF officials gave both men a chance to beat the champion.

Illustrated. Denying Luger would be like denying the fans.

Luger had every intention of making the most of his opportunity in the Royal Rumble. After Luger had eliminated Shawn Michaels and Bret Hart was able to eliminate Fatu, Luger and Hart were the last two men remaining. Luger and Hart slugged it out in the center of the ring. Both men were desperate to get the coveted title shot. Then Hart and Luger got tangled in the ropes, went over the top, and hit the floor at the same time. Referees Joey Marella and Dave Hebner argued about who had hit the floor first. Ring announcer Howard Finkel announced that Luger had won. After Marella and Hebner talked some more, Finkel announced that Hart had won. Minutes later, WWF President Jack Tunney walked to the ring, conferred with Marella and Hebner, and declared Hart and Luger cowinners.

Who would get the title shot? Nobody knew. There couldn't be two number one contenders to the world title. Both men couldn't wrestle Yokozuna at WrestleMania X . . . or could they?

Tunney's decision shocked the wrestling world . . . and Yokozuna. The world champion would defend his title twice at WrestleMania— once against Hart and once against Luger.

A coin flip was held to decide who would wrestle first. The outcome was crucial. One man would be able to wrestle fresh against a champion who had already competed. Hart won the coin flip and would wrestle the second match against Yokozuna.

WrestleMania X was held on March 20 at Madison Square Garden in New York. The first main event was Luger vs. Yokozuna with Curt

"Mr. Perfect" Hennig as special guest referee. Luger wrestled a great match, but couldn't control his emotions. Twice in the first three minutes, Luger tried for pins when Yokozuna hadn't been worn down nearly enough. Yokozuna took control of the match and worked on Luger's shoulders with nerve pinches and chops. With under 10 minutes gone, Yokozuna tossed Luger out of the ring and into a steel barrier. Luger returned to the ring, but Yokozuna slammed him to the mat.

Luger blocked a punch, then rammed Yokozuna's head into the turnbuckle. Three clotheslines sent Yokozuna crashing to the mat with a giant thud. Now Luger was ready to go in for the kill. Yokozuna was helpless. Cornette climbed onto the ring apron. Luger flipped Cornette into the ring, then hooked Yokozuna's legs and covered him for nine seconds, during which Hennig wouldn't make the count. Luger stood up and pushed Hennig, then covered Yokozuna again. Hennig called for the bell and disqualified Luger.

"I called it as I saw it, and that was right down the middle," Hennig said afterward. "He has no business putting his hands on 'Mr. Perfect' or any official of the WWF. It's an automatic disqualification. One, you don't throw a manager into the ring and, two, you don't touch an official."

Luger got in Hennig's face. "It's bogus and you know it," he said.

Later in the night, Hart beat Yokozuna to win the world title, and Luger graciously shook "the Hitman's" hand.

Luger kept winning matches. He used his human torture rack to beat Rick Martel, Bam

Bam Bigelow, Irwin R. Schyster, and Crush during a three-day period. He beat Jeff Jarrett by submission. Luger and Bret even teamed to beat Yokozuna and Owen Hart. But Luger became sidetracked by a feud with Crush, and put his title hopes aside. He tried to win the intercontinental title from Diesel, but he was frustrated by disqualifications and double-countouts. Luger was also sidetracked by a feud with Tatanka.

By late 1994, Luger's popularity had waned and he found it difficult to get title shots. Determined to keep his career alive, Luger left the WCW and returned to the WWF.

Suddenly, Luger found himself out of title contention. At SummerSlam '94, Bret Hart defended his world title against Owen Hart. Razor Ramon won the intercontinental title from Diesel. And Luger suffered a stunning loss to Tatanka. In October, Luger stepped forward when former world champion Bob Backlund boasted that nobody could escape his chicken wing submission hold. Luger was getting the best of Backlund in their match, but Tatanka interfered, and Backlund locked on his chicken wing. Later in the card, Tatanka attacked Luger in the locker room while he was being interviewed by Vince McMahon Jr.

Luger begged for title shots. He sent a letter to WWF President Jack Tunney saying he wanted to wrestle the winner of the match between world champion Bret Hart and Backlund at the Survivor Series. His request was ignored. His war with Tatanka raged on. On November 9 in Bethlehem, Pennsylvania, Tatanka kicked and punched Luger, but Lex battled back. They wrestled in and out of the ring before Luger placed Tatanka in the torture rack. Tatanka refused to submit. Owen Hart interfered and attacked Luger.

Through it all, Luger continued to be passed over for title shots, despite beating Jerry Lawler, Tatanka, Irwin R. Schyster, and King Kong Bundy all in the same week. Instead of getting world champion Diesel, he got Tatanka, again and again and again. His career was stuck on a treadmill. Grudge matches were getting him nowhere.

Luger started sinking in the WWF ratings. He wrestled in the opening match at WrestleMania XI on April 2, 1995, in Hartford,

Connecticut, teaming with Davey Boy Smith to beat Jacob and Eli Blu. The match was meaningless. He bombed out in the King of the Ring tournament, losing to Yokozuna by countout in a qualifying match. By that time, he had dropped entirely out of the WWF ratings.

The man who had saved America from Yokozuna, the man who had traveled the country on the Lex Express, the man who had said he would win the WWF World title, was far from glory. With his WWF career going nowhere, Luger searched for options. Finally, on September 4, 1995, he chose the most obvious option: a return to WCW. Luger did a good job keeping the move secret. He appeared at WWF TV tapings on August 28 and 29 and was scheduled to appear at several WWF arena cards in September.

"I'd been asking the WWF for title shots for months," Luger told *Pro Wrestling Illustrated Weekly.* "It got frustrating. I wasn't getting the matches I wanted, and then with Davey Boy Smith going with Jim Cornette, I needed a change. My head was spinning after all that's happened, and nothing positive was happening."

That changed in a hurry. Luger showed up at the September 4 broadcast of *WCW Monday Nitro* in Minneapolis dressed in street clothes, then walked down the aisle to watch a few seconds of Ric Flair's match against Sting. Thirty minutes later, Luger helped Hulk Hogan, who was being attacked by Kevin Sullivan, Kamala, Shark, Zodiac, and Meng. Luger and Hogan cleared the ring, but collided.

"What are you doing here?" Hogan asked Luger.

"I'm sick of wrestling kids," Luger said. "I want a shot at the WCW World title."

Hogan promised Luger a shot at the title at the next *Nitro*. The two exchanged words and shoves before leaving the ring. Most of the fans cheered Luger and booed Hogan.

It hadn't taken much for Luger to get the world title opportunity he wanted. All he had to do was go home.

BACK IN WCW

Although Luger fell short in his match against WCW World champion Hulk Hogan at *WCW Monday Nitro* on September 11, 1995 (losing by disqualification after Kevin Sullivan, Shark, Meng, Kamala, and Zodiac interfered), he soared in the ratings. Within weeks of his return to WCW, he was the number two contender to the world title.

Luger's career had been topsy-turvy from the start. He seemingly could never decide whether he wanted to be a fan favorite or a rulebreaker. Since returning to WCW, he had been a fan favorite allied with Hogan and manager Jimmy Hart. But all that changed at Halloween Havoc on October 29, 1995.

First, Luger had a strange match against Meng. Kevin Sullivan was at ringside for Meng, but every time Luger was thrown from the ring, Sullivan whispered encouragement to Luger instead of kicking him. When Meng had Luger pinned, Sullivan interfered and got Luger disqualified.

Later in the night, Hogan was on the verge of beating the Giant when Hart climbed onto the ring apron and slugged referee Randy Anderson. Hart acted like he didn't know what happened, then hit Hogan with the world title belt. The Giant and Yeti joined in the attack on Hogan. Then Luger and Savage walked to the ring. Luger kicked Savage, then the

Once a target of the NWO, Luger joined forces with the rulebreaking clique in 1999.

At 7' 4" and 430 pounds, WCW World champion the Giant stood a foot taller than Lex and outweighed him by 160 pounds.

Giant helped Luger put Hogan in the torture rack. Luger released Hogan and placed Savage in the torture rack.

"Did you see it?" Luger told reporters. "Hogan never saw it coming. He never felt the rack like he did tonight. Hogan tasted death in my arms, and it's only gonna get worse."

The world title was declared vacant because of Hart's interference. Luger concentrated on becoming a two-time world champion in the 60-man, three-ring battle royal at World War III on November 26 in Norfolk, Virginia. With 27 minutes gone in the match, only Luger, Hogan, Savage, Ric Flair, Arn Anderson, the Giant, Sting, and One Man Gang remained. Then Flair and Anderson were eliminated. Luger and Sting double-teamed the Giant, but Hogan made his way to where they were battling and shoved all three men over the top rope. Savage went on to win the world title.

Luger took another shot at the world title at Starrcade on December 27 in Nashville, Tennessee. Luger, Sting, and Ric Flair battled first in a triangle match to determine who would face Savage later in the evening. The rules for the triangle match were that only two men could be in the ring at the same time, but the third man could be tagged in by either of the other wrestlers. Flair spent the first 17 minutes of the match in the ring, but was on the ring apron when Luger lifted Sting into his torture rack with 26 minutes gone. While he was above Luger's head, Sting's foot slammed into the referee and knocked him out. Flair knocked both Sting and Luger to the arena floor. The referee regained consciousness and counted out Sting and Luger. Flair was the winner. Minutes later, he beat Savage for the world title.

Luger's frustration was building. He had returned to WCW with the specific goal of winning the world title, and now it looked as if he would fall short again. But instead of moaning about his fate, Luger went after the WCW World tag team title.

On January 22, 1996, in Las Vegas, Luger and Sting battled world champions Booker T and Stevie Ray of Harlem Heat. Late in the match, Jimmy Hart handed Luger a roll of coins. Luger struck Booker T with the coins, sending his opponent to the mat, then scored the pin for the title. Boasted Luger, "There's not a single team on this planet we can't beat."

As champions, though, Sting and Luger didn't have to win. All they had to do was not get pinned. They lost to the Nasty Boys by disqualification, but retained the title. At SuperBrawl VI, Sting and Luger battled the Road Warriors to a no-contest. Luger added another title to his trophy chest on February 17, 1996, by beating Johnny B. Badd for the WCW TV title. Badd regained the belt from Luger one day later, but Luger won it again on March 6, starting a title reign of five months, two weeks.

Luger and Sting defended the world tag title against Flair and the Giant in an unusual match at *WCW Monday Nitro* on April 22 in Albany, Georgia. The tag belts weren't the only titles on the line. If Flair got pinned, he would lose the world heavyweight title to whoever pinned him. If Luger got pinned, he would lose the TV title to whoever pinned him.

But nobody got pinned. Sting and Luger won by disqualification when Flair took a cup of hot coffee from Woman, a female wrestler, and threw it toward Sting and Luger. The tag champs moved out of the way and the coffee hit the Giant in the eyes.

Sting and Luger, however, had a hard time getting along. Perhaps it was impossible to form an alliance between two men who had the same goal: the WCW World heavyweight title. When Sting was granted more matches than Luger

Outsider Razor Ramon squeezes Luger in a headlock. In 1996, Ramon and his friend Kevin Nash invaded WCW and sought to take over the federation, but they were stymied by loyal WCW wrestlers like Luger, Sting, and Randy Savage.

against new world champion the Giant, Luger protested.

"I am very happy for Sting, but I'm a WCW tag team champion and the TV champion," Luger told *Pro Wrestling Illustrated Weekly.* "I've earned my shots, too."

Replied Sting: "When I win the belt, I'll give him the first title match. This isn't even worth getting upset about. He'll have his chances."

Luger wasn't willing to be patient. He interfered in Sting's match against the Giant at Slamboree '96, enabling the Giant to defend the title. The Luger-Sting world tag team title reign ended on June 24, 1996, in a triangle tag team match involving Harlem Heat and Rick and Scott Steiner. Harlem Heat regained the belts.

Luger got his chance at the world heavyweight title against the Giant at the Great American Bash on June 16 in Baltimore. Before the match, Luger said he had a secret plan to place the Giant in his torture rack. That figured to be no easy task: the Giant is 7' 4" and 430 pounds.

"I'll wait for the Giant to make a mistake, which he will, and then I'll make my move," Luger vowed. The Giant did make a mistake. Luger did place the Giant in the torture rack, but Luger couldn't sustain the hold long enough. Moments later, the Giant chokeslammed Luger for the pin.

Meanwhile, bigger things were happening in WCW than mere battles over world titles. The federation was undergoing a substantial change. Scott Hall and Kevin Nash, known in the WWF as Razor Ramon and Diesel, had invaded WCW as the Outsiders. Their goal was to take over WCW from the inside. At Bash at the Beach on July 7, 1996, in Daytona Beach, Florida, Luger, Sting, and Savage defended the honor of WCW against Hall, Nash, and a mystery man, whom Hall and Nash said was a former WWF star.

The identity of the mystery man was not revealed until late in the match. After injuring his knee, Luger was carried from the ring on a stretcher. Hogan walked down the runway to the ring. Most people thought he was coming to help Sting and Savage, but Hogan legdropped Savage and high-fived Nash and Hall.

Wrestling had seen the debut of the NWO, a clique that would change the sport.

Now Luger didn't have a choice between being considered a rulebreaker or a fan favorite. Anybody who wasn't with the NWO was a fan favorite, and Luger definitely wasn't with the NWO.

At Hog Wild on August 10, Sting and Luger teamed again but lost to Hall and Nash. The NWO was taking over. Hogan regained the world title from the Giant. The WCW wrestlers joined forces to fight off the NWO's invasion. At Clash of the Champions XXXIII, a triangle match involving Luger and Sting, Harlem Heat, and Rick and Scott Steiner was stopped because Hall and Nash attacked Luger and Sting at ringside.

Luger was one of the NWO's prime targets. On August 20, Luger defended the TV title against Lord Steven Regal. Luger was dominating the match when Hall and Nash marched to ringside. When Luger was outside the ring, Hall and Nash slammed him into a ringpost and rolled him into the ring. Regal made the pin.

"That belt meant a lot to our buddy Lex, so the NWO decided he couldn't have it anymore," Nash said. "When the NWO puts their mind to something, we get it done. We have the NWO World title, and we made sure Luger lost the TV title."

The NWO vs. WCW feud intensified at Fall Brawl '96. Luger, Flair, Arn Anderson, and Sting battled Nash, Hogan, Hall, and an impostor Sting in the War Games main event. The WCW team lost when Luger submitted to the impostor Sting's scorpion deathlock.

"The NWO isn't going to last," Luger told *Pro Wrestling Illustrated Weekly*. "We're seeing it start to crack already. We might destroy them or they might destroy themselves. There are too many egos in there as it is. It'll be a true pleasure watching the immortal Hulk Hogan and all his lackeys go down in flames."

Luger was at the front line of the NWO vs. WCW battle. In the World War III battle royal, Luger, the Giant, Nash, Hall, and Six were the last five men remaining. Luger eliminated Hall and Six, but was shoved out of the ring by the Giant as he was eliminating Nash.

Elizabeth, Randy Savage's ex-wife and valet, reappeared on the wrestling scene in 1999 as Lex Luger's rulebreaking assistant. Never afraid to interfere on Luger's behalf, Elizabeth helped him to win matches.

A hand injury nearly prevented Luger from joining the Giant in a match against WCW World tag team champions Scott Hall and Kevin Nash. The Giant wrestled the entire match on his own, until Luger came out in street clothes, tagged the Giant, and forced Nash to submit to his signature "torture rack" backbreaker. Luger and the Giant, however, did not get the tag team title.

Luger suffered another setback when his Team WCW lost to Team NWO at Uncensored on March 16, 1997. With the victory, the NWO was entitled to demand a shot at any WCW title whenever it pleased.

Luger bounced back at Spring Stampede in a four-way match that also involved Stevie Ray, the Giant, and Booker T. At stake was a shot at the WCW World title, and Luger won it by forcing Stevie Ray to submit to his torture rack. Luger, however, again fell short in his title bid against Hogan, and had to settle for a moral victory when he forced Hogan to submit to his backbreaker on June 9, 1997. The victory was impressive: Hogan hadn't submitted in 16 years.

"He'll never do it again," Hogan vowed.

Hogan was wrong. At Bash at the Beach on July 13, 1997, Luger teamed with the Giant against Hogan and National Basketball Association (NBA) star Dennis Rodman. As the Giant held off an attack by an impostor Sting, Luger lifted Hogan into his torture rack and got another submission victory.

"Hogan, there's no way you can get away with not giving me the title shot I rightfully deserve," Luger said. "I racked you twice on television. Now I'm coming to get that belt from you, and there's nothing your gang of thugs can do about it."

Replied Hogan: "Luger can keep saying he deserves a title shot all he wants. I'll give him one when I'm good and ready, and I'm not ready yet."

WCW officials made the decision for him. On August 4, 1997, Hogan was forced to defend the title against Luger at *WCW Monday Nitro.* Luger was ready. Despite interference from Hall, Nash, and Savage, Luger placed Hogan in his torture rack and won by submission to capture his second world title. It was an impressive victory by Luger. But the NWO couldn't be denied. Five days later at Road Wild, the NWO again interfered, and an attack by a bat-wielding impostor Sting led to Hogan pinning Luger and regaining the title.

"I did everything I could," Luger said, "but one man can only do so much against a gang attack, especially when one of the guys in the gang has a baseball bat. Hogan can't beat me without help from his goons."

Dallas Page joined Luger in the battle against the NWO. They were the heroes of WCW, but the NWO couldn't be denied. They were too big, too strong, and too ruthless. At Starrcade '97, Luger suffered a humiliating defeat to another NWO member, Marcus "Buff" Bagwell. Luger dropped in the WCW ratings. But the fans hadn't lost their respect for the "Total Package": He was voted Wrestler of the Year by the readers of *Pro Wrestling Illustrated* magazine.

"This is the ultimate validation for me," Luger said. "In some ways, I felt I let WCW and the fans down when Hogan beat me. But for the people to recognize me with this honor makes up for everything. I knew I had their support, but now I know I have their trust."

In the middle of 1998, a split between Nash and Hogan resulted in the forming of two NWOs: NWO Wolfpac, led by Nash, and NWO Hollywood, led by Hogan. Almost all of the top wrestlers found themselves on one side or the other. Luger and Sting joined with Hennig, Konnan, and Nash in the Wolfpac.

Although the feud between NWO Hollywood and the Wolfpac was hot, Luger seemed to be running in quicksand, fighting meaningless feuds and getting few title shots of any kind. Sure, he had some good stretches, such as the week in November 1998 when he beat Hall three times and the Giant once. "Can a shot at Bill Goldberg's WCW World title be far off? Not if Luger continues his winning ways," surmised *Pro Wrestling Illustrated Weekly.*

A world title shot was on the line in the battle royal at World War III. Hall, Nash, and Luger were the last three men remaining, but it was Nash, not Luger, who eliminated both men to earn the shot at Goldberg.

"I expected to win it myself," said Luger, who was clearly peeved by the outcome.

This time, Luger refused to make himself an NWO outcast. When the group reunited as one at the turn of the year, Luger was among the group's members, along with Hogan, Hall, Nash, Scott Steiner, and Bagwell. He was a member of the group he had resisted for so long. Not for long. On January 30, 1999, during a singles match against Konnan, Luger tore a tendon in his left arm. He was sidelined for the next five months.

By the time Luger returned to the ring, the NWO was history and Sting was deciding whether to align with Hulk Hogan. Luger kept telling Sting that Hogan couldn't be trusted. Sting warned Luger not to interfere in his title match against Hogan at Fall Brawl on September 12, 1999, but it turned out it was Luger who couldn't be trusted. He handed Sting a baseball bat, which Sting used to slug Hogan and score the pin. Sting and Luger hugged after the match.

Sting and Luger were a team again, at least for a while. At *Nitro* on October 18, Luger hit Bret Hart with a baseball bat, enabling Sting to win. Later in the month, Elizabeth—Randy Savage's former wife and valet—shocked the wrestling world by returning to the sport at *Nitro* and handing a baseball bat to Luger, who used the bat to help Sting beat Hart and Flair. Most fans didn't know that Luger and Elizabeth were dating.

As had happened before, the Sting-Luger alliance couldn't last. They started arguing. Luger tried to clear things up, but Sting refused his apology. At *Nitro* on November 8, during Sting's match against Goldberg, Luger knocked out the referee and sprayed Mace in Sting's face. Sting got revenge by pinning Luger the next week. Luger interfered and hit Sting with a bat during one of Sting's matches against Bret Hart. Sting and Luger brawled again at *Nitro* on November 29. A week after that, Elizabeth signed a contract stating that she was Sting's manager. Luger, disguised as Sting, attacked "Diamond" Dallas Page; later, Page attacked the real Sting, as Luger—the impostor Sting—was seen running from the building.

When Luger came to the ring disguised as Sting, Sting placed him in a torture rack. At Starrcade '99, Elizabeth turned against Sting and helped Luger win.

Luger was in the midst of chaotic events, and once again became a full-fledged rule-breaker. Elizabeth was his partner in crime. Elizabeth's interference enabled Luger to place Booker T in his torture rack at *Nitro* on January 24, 2000. Luger insulted Hogan at *Nitro* on February 7 and broke Jimmy Hart's hand with a chair.

The "Total Package" was ruthless.

On February 14, 2000, Luger used a steel chair to break Terry Funk's hand. Later in the night, Luger prevented Hogan from pinning Flair, then leveled Hogan with a baseball bat. Luger and Flair were a team: Team Package.

As boastful as he was as the Narcissist, Luger was now more conceited than ever. He called himself the greatest physical specimen in pro wrestling. He boasted about how Hogan was washed up. At *Nitro* on February 21, an attack by Luger and Flair left Hogan unconscious. Two weeks later, Luger and Flair conspired to break Curt Hennig's wrist. Time and again, Sting had to sprint to the ring to save the victims of Luger's and Flair's attacks.

Sting and Luger battled in a lumberjack match at Uncensored on March 19, 2000. Sting was ready to finish off Luger when Elizabeth hit him with a baseball bat. Luger placed Sting in a torture rack, but Vampiro saved Sting, who scored the pin.

Vampiro became Luger's main target. Flair, Luger, and Elizabeth unleashed a brutal baseball bat attack on Vampiro at *Nitro*, until Sting

Though they have been both friends and enemies in the wrestling ring, Luger, left, and Sting, right, are friends in real life. The two wrestlers were caught in a headlock by 11-year-old Ryan Loepke during a promotional event at Planet Hollywood in Las Vegas. Sting and Luger were helping to raise money for the Childhood Cancer Foundation.

made the save. At *Nitro* on March 27, Sting and Vampiro defeated Luger and Flair in a Texas Tornado match. Sting and Luger brawled to a hotel pool, where Sting blocked a piledriver and backdropped Luger into the water. Luger and Sting continued their fight on the beach, and then in the ocean. Finally, Sting backdropped Luger and scored the pin.

Despite losing that match, Luger was hot stuff. Fourteen years after making his WCW debut, Luger was still a main event wrestler in WCW. But, once again, things were about to change in WCW. A total restructuring of the federation took place in early April. WCW executives Vince Russo and Eric Bischoff ushered in a new era for the federation, in which the younger wrestlers—the New Blood—would get priority over the veteran wrestlers—the

Millionaires Club. Luger was part of the Millionaires Club.

The emergence of the New Blood halted any momentum Luger had gained. Russo and Bischoff set out to destroy the veteran wrestlers, and Russo went so far as to gain control of Elizabeth's contract. For several months, Elizabeth was forced to do whatever Russo wanted. Luger tried to get her back, but Russo's contract was ironclad. Elizabeth couldn't escape.

Russo and Bischoff called the shots, and when Luger and Elizabeth kept complaining about the situation, both of them were sent home for five months. Team Package was history.

Luger, however, couldn't stay away from wrestling. In the fall of 2000, he returned to the ring and set his sights on Bill Goldberg. As the first year of the new millennium ended, the feud between Goldberg and Luger was heating up. Once again, Luger finds himself in the spotlight . . . a place he has rarely left for the past 15 years.

It's a place he is likely to occupy for a long time to come.

Chronology

1958   Born Larry Pfhol in Chicago on June 2

1985   Makes his pro debut as Lex Luger on October 31; defeats Wahoo McDaniel for the southern title on November 19

1985   Defeats Wahoo McDaniel for the southern title

1986   Named Rookie of the Year by *Pro Wrestling Illustrated* magazine

1987   Wins his first U.S. title, from Nikita Koloff on July 11

1988   With Barry Windham, defeats Tully Blanchard and Arn Anderson for the NWA World tag team title on March 27; teams with Sting to win the Jim Crockett Sr. Memorial Cup Tag Team Tournament on April 22 and 23

1989   Defeats Barry Windham for his second U.S. title on February 20; loses the belt to Michael Hayes on May 7; wins the belt back from Hayes for his third U.S. title on May 22

1991   Defeats Barry Windham for the WCW World heavyweight title on July 14

1992   Loses the WCW World title to Sting on February 29

1993   Bodyslams WWF World champion Yokozuna at the "Stars & Stripes Challenge" on July 4

1995   Returns to WCW on September 4

1996   Teams with Sting to win the WCW World tag team title from Harlem Heat on January 22

1997   Hulk Hogan defeats Luger for the WCW World heavyweight title on August 9

1999   Tears a tendon in his left arm on January 30 and is sidelined for five months

2000   Forms Team Package with Ric Flair on February 14 and feuds with Hulk Hogan

Further Reading

Anderson, Steve. "The Rack Is Back! `Hogan Tasted Death in My Arms!'" *Wrestling Superstars* (Spring 1996): 39-41.

Burkett, Harry. "Hogan–Bret–Sting–Luger: Who Can You Trust? None of Them!" *Pro Wrestling Illustrated* (February 2000): 32-34.

"Ric Flair: 'Lex Luger Is Wearing Me Down.'" *Inside Wrestling* (December 1988): 30-33.

"Luger Wins WCW Title; Race Now His Manager." *Pro Wrestling Illustrated Weekly* (July 29, 1991): 1.

Rosenbaum, David. "Forecast for Lex Luger: Reign Ending!" *Pro Wrestling Illustrated* (April 1992): 35-37.

Index

Photo Credits

JACQUELINE MUDGE is a frequent contributor to sports and entertainment magazines in the United States. Born in Idaho, she became a wrestling fan at age 11 when her father took her to matches. Although she has a degree in journalism, she left the writing arena for several years in the late 1980s to pursue a career in advertising sales. She returned to the profession—and the sport she loves—in 1995. Her previously published volumes on the mat sport include *Randy Savage: The Story of the Wrestler They Call "Macho Man"* and *Bret Hart: The Story of the Wrestler They Call "The Hitman."*